ODDITY/LER:
SCORPION /EAGLE
PHOENIX /

pain, power, glory

I release an arrow of light
to arc silently through the darkness

This will be an explosion of mental brilliance
Against all that heavy pain

I'm just passing through this life
before I pass away
Pass or Fail,
Moving So Fast through time
I might pass out

Even without the dumb rainbow flag from the gays

or the fantastical coat of many colors back from the holy days
I can pass with FLYING COLORS

Pure Child of February,
Today you will be the one to MARCH,

ISBN: 978-0-578-64804-0
Fonts by Jess Latham.
Thank You.

Printed, Distributed and Bound in the United States of America
First Printing 02/20/2020

Published by
He Who Rebels Against All
Oklahoma City, Oklahoma
73106

Hey, Thanks for getting a copy!
I wanted to take on the whole world -
- buying one of my books really means the world to me.

Facebook.com/TylerLazarus1992

Facebook.com/Oddityler

The Direction of YOUR ERECTION

TLS
By Tyler Lazarus Stump

DANCE WITH ME BABY, DANCE WITH **AN ENTITY AS DARK+INSANE** AS ME
JUST FOR ONE NIGHT

I have said what needed to be said,
I have said what has never been said

Writ upon the fiery wings of near insane angels
Mind of mine to confer spinning down to the earth,
Here I stand humbled before the tide of time
As greater and lesser men have come with their thoughts to the dais
before I, in birth, had reached it
Take this mental offering, typed in black assertiveness
All my pain, silent suffering, of disapproval and eyes
watching
All the oath <u>for ten years</u> that has been mine.

Take this weighty burden,
and somehow make it fly.

Give me unstoppable spiritual light, for a time,
to outshine
ALL the strange, dark things they believe.
Now I explode out
In an inferno of truth, a historical echo
to sound through the historical record
Paragraphs of lies, verbal slander and unfair falsehood
All these holy books,
no wonder nobody is on the same page
I'll have to be that of a man, I'll have to be of a woman
Protected with sacred cloth of the sisterhood
In the Holy Neighborhood
I challenge them with THE POWER OF my manhood
Woven Words A, Flame
against all the lies
A LIGHTHOUSE
T Y L E R BECOMES KNOWN
AS A POWERHOUSE

In the next life,
They promise me fire,
IN THIS LIFE
Show them NOW who has actually the real firepower.
Their God and Devil will fall before me.
I have reached the end,
but I have a strange feeling
that this is only a beginning.

The camera watching catches quick glimpses of a Scorpion Necklace,
Eagle Feathers in my hair,
and a Tattoo of a phoenix on my wrist

**I leave one defining statement burning
behind
in the sands of time:**

*DEFY CONVENTION
THROUGH INVENTION*

02/22/92

The Direction Of Your Erection ⚋
Part 1 - The Scorpion

EVERY sociologist and their acclaimed illiterate mother has tried to take a shot at this.
Every preacher, philosopher, politician, psychologist - every person on Facebook.
And everyone has missed the mark. Completely rapid misfires.

10,000 arrows from intense, very opinionated attempts and nobody hit that cultural bullseye.

If they had, then I wouldn't have had to DO it.

I wouldn't have spent the better part of a decade watching the world turn, and closely observing how people felt + thought around/about a group of people, and HOW that group of people maneuvered themselves through historical debris of corrupted, dogmatic, insane Thinking. I mean religion.

What is homosexuality? What does it mean? What is it REALLY?
Aberration? Sin? Social Defect?

WRONG
NO
FAKE NEWS

none of y'all can aim for shit.

Jesus christ.

Give me the fuckin bow.

I got this god damn thing.

takes aim

+pulls bow string back+

focuses

releases

smiles

A BULLSEYE
FOR ALL THE BULLSHIT:

Watches Homosexuals and Christians argue, and yell at each other. Looks at the "Born Again Believers" Fight Against The "Born This Way."

For the LIFE of me, you both have brought a plague of death and ignorance to this issue.

Looks at the Posters, Sees the Bible Verses

Grabs Forehead in an intense Migraine

SHUTUP!

SHUTUP!

SHUTUP!

ALL OF YOU - GAY PEOPLE AND RELIGIOUS PEOPLE -

SHUT. THE. HELL. UP.

1.OKAY.
Now that you've shut up:
Listen up.
Drop your stupid ass rainbow flags and your bible verses right here.
Neither will be serving us. We don't need either of them.

SETS THE BIBLE ON FIRE,
SETS THE RAINBOW FLAG ON FIRE,

sets them both on fire as the homosexual and the christian scream in shock and horror

Watches the pages burn and the flag turn to ashes

HOW DARE YOU - scream the christians
HOW DAERTH YOU - lisps the homosexuals

Deal with it, dummies
Because I need to you put all that other shit aside, and JUST LISTEN to me for the next half hour.
JUST. LISTEN.

Fellow homosexual - *you are guilty of making a total fool of yourself and thinking that wearing unicorn hats and being half naked was going to help push the gears of society forward. WHAT EVEN. Society didn't need your naked body, it needed your mind. But you were too content to walk around with your ding dong flopping obscenely out in the street, paired with stupid rainbow socks; making a "statement."*

~~UGH.~~
~~FACEPALM~~

Christian - *you're just guilty of not using ANY critical thinking on this, but I suppose in the spirit of your christ all can eventually be forgiven. Despite the fact* *that innumerable lives were lived out in shame and pain. Or far worse. All because of a book. If one book actually did all this damage, it'll take another (well written) one to UNDO it all.*

~~JESUS.~~
~~NAPALM~~

Both of you idiots have given me a headache. DELETE IT.

Let's begin.

Being gay has NOTHING to do with what you think it has to do with.

Not the bible verses, not the scriptures, not "Sodom and Gomorrah."

None of that crap. NONE.

Here's the truth.

Hello...

Taps microphone tip

Is this thing on?

Looks at the horde of curious people, now watching me
clears throat, self-consciously

This will be a defining contribution.
I leave something of monumental importance behind.

HELOOOOOOOOoooo
CAN---YOU----ALL---HEAR----ME?

Good.

After reading what I am about to say, homosexuality will forever be easily explained away. F O R E V E R. IN PERPETUITY. ETERNALLY. That sentence is in bold - but this is not just another bold claim. *SLAMS GAVEL DOWN*

And a lot of the lingering issues that still surround it, will begin to dissipate. **Hopefully.** I need this to get filtered into the public water supply - without actually watering any of it down - which is why I'll be keeping the price so cheap and giving away as many free versions as I can.

I'll be throwing this book/paper at people's heads.

READ IT.

People need to hear this. Le Screw the whole literary world. I'm not doing this to rub shoulders with the pulitzer prize winners or book festival comities.
This is for everyday people out there with gay family members and friends, acquaintances, etc... to understand.

Your Socially Awkward Male Cousin who has suspiciously never had a girlfriend, because he's "focusing on school" (Lmao)--- this book is for YOU to understand HIM, or her, WHATEVER!

What I am about to do - It's never been explained this way, which is why I'm taking this route.

The answer **lies** within the **truth** of these pages.

We're keeping it short, because we're ALREADY super short for time.
The social damage and scarification has already been done in a million different forms.
Now I have to clean up the *entire* **fucking mess**.
OF TWO THOUSAND YEARS!!!

Speed, Efficiency, Thoroughness, Accuracy.
Lets do this quick, lets do it well, lets get it done, correctly. So we never have to do or say any of this AGAIN.

I'm not EVEN going to expound upon all the gay suicide, gay killing and bullying that has already happened, the LGBTQ-ABCDEFG Blah, blah blah bullshit
Or remark all that much on the Pulse shooting, hangings, all that messed up stuff that's happened and been processed as history in American culture. Wah-Wah-Wah No bully stories, No "I killed myself" because I was gay and nobody accepted me.

This is not that book.

There is no use crying over spilt milk, or spilt souls.
or dead gay boys.

I can't alter or amend the horror show of past, so it's best for brevity's sake to focus on the present moment and the moment leading into the future.

I CANT BRING BACK THE DEAD

I chose a biblical name, because I have wounds of Biblical ORIGIN.

TYLER.
LAZARUS.
STUMP.

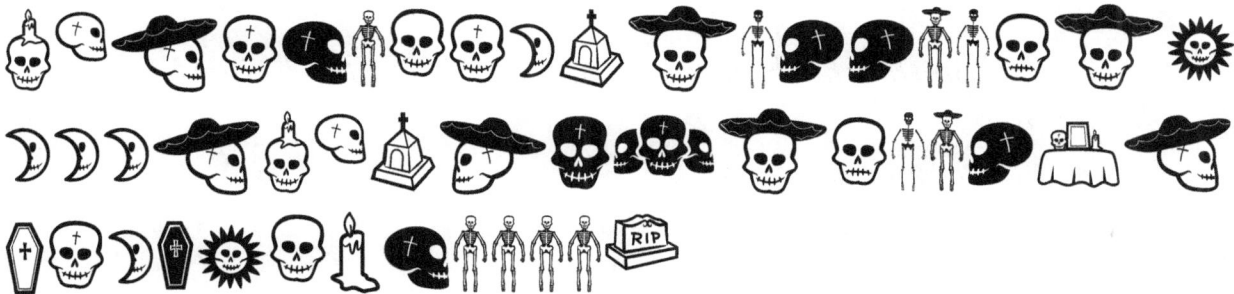

*BUT I ALSO WONT LET HUMAN HISTORY ALA
ANNE FRANK-ENSTEIN ME!*

Before publishing this, years ago,
I wrote a 450 page book 11.5 x 8 (it looked like a HUGE phonebook), complete with

diagrams and poetry and any every other flavor of ideas I had at the time,
to hit the issue from any possibly angle, it ended up hitting the Amazon bestseller list for
a week, and I was next to James Franco, a celebrity,
who was writing a poetry book about being gay.
A cool moment to see myself from, from the efforts of my own will and stubbornness,
succeeding on the publishing front, but writing isnt my true calling,
even though I am writing now.
Dont ask, Dont Telephone.

SO! Here we go.

cracks knuckles

We all know what the Bible, (and also what every other religious text) has to say on the
subject.

Yes, Yes, yes **eternal damnation, won't inherit the kingdom of god, whipped by 1,000
demons, all that jazz**

(all that jizz)

But the key to unlocking this forbidden door, has nothing to do with Christianity,
although Christianity is what has persecuted it and preceded it.

It has nothing to do with the Bible, God, Moses, Jesus, Mohammed.

It has to do with my big, dangling WEINER.

*draws a penis on the chalkboard, complete with pubic hair AND
matching balls*
Stares at it for a split second

thinks about making it even bigger
half-shrugs

Good enough

Let the record show <u>that every other person</u> that tried to tackle and give diligence to
this topic, tragically missed the mark by a fair margin.

That isn't to denigrate their work or ideas, at a wholesale level, but that the undeniable truth hasn't ever been possessed so far by anyone in history or any other sociological page.

We've been around (as a species) for about 200,000 years.
It's taken THAT long for someone - A HOMO SEXUAL THATS A HOMO SAPIEN - to say this. It's so obvious it's painful that it's been overlooked and hidden for SO LONG.

We've gotten the hard stuff out of the way, so let me explain about other things that GET HARD.

erases the flaccid penis

Being gay, has nothing to do with what people STILL THINK it has to do with.

No dances with lucifer at midnight, no background sexual abuse,
No lack of strong, central male figures, no illuminati meetings (sadly, I wish)
No Red Devil whispering blasphemy into my ear, as a Beatles record plays backwards.

It has nothing to do with the rainbow, or glitter, or unicorns, or anything prescribed.
There isn't anything wrong with that, but I do shake my head at the multitude of missteps that happened along the way to get up to this point,
when THIS point - meaning gay marriage and gay tolerance - could have been reached a far quicker rate with the aid of a cohesive and succinct message to stand behind,
instead of yelling and walking in a poorly sewn mermaid costume down the street and yelling *I WAS BORN THIS WAY.*

Fools. Born a damn fool.
And then you tried doing all THAT stuff in front of "Born Again" Christians. Oh my god.

Of course being naked with your junk out
- in a leather BDSM Harness -

BACKFIRED.

*CHRIST/OPHER ON A CROSS *Facepalms**

But then all the gays wonder why nobody took them and their cause seriously. CAUSE you look like pornography when you're trying to land something, politically (and even MORE importantly, philosophically.) DUR…DUR…DUR

You meant well, but you didn't succeed at the target objective quite so well.
You argued, you screamed, you ranted, you wrote your social media posts, (I saw them; I read them)
You still failed, because had you succeeded what lingered - in differing forms of social pressure - wouldn't still remain.

HAD ANYONE SAID WHAT IM ABOUT TO SAY,
THEN I WOULDN'T HAVE HAD TO SAY IT

The problem, or **the main problem**, is that homosexuality, a sociological and sexual condition has become embedded, entwined and twisted into the battle of religious rhetoric,
which in itself has twisted itself even more.

Religion of the same idea can't even agree with ITSELF. It's why their are splits, schisms of thought and differing denominations. Take a completely unrelated issue and throw it into the mix - being gay - and you have a real fucking disaster waiting to unfold. Which it did.

Look how many strong and diverse opinions people have had on it.
People who aren't gay have had so much to say about it.
So much that was just flat out W R O N G.

Homosexuality is an issue in a layer of knots. It's always been like a knotted up pair of headphones, wrapped in messy and hard to remove layers of even more complicated knots.

It's 2020, and it's time to unravel those knots.

WE ARE AT A STALEMATE,
OF OPINIONS THAT HAVE BECOME STALE.

I don't even need to argue about love, or feelings.
In fact, emotion can be taken right out of the equation on this.

This has never been put into print, it's never been talked about,
but here we go.

This is the simple, undeniable, incontrovertible truth.

ARE YOU READY? ARE YOU REALLY READY???

ARE YOU FREAKIN READY, BABY????

<u>My dick cannot get hard - looking at a naked woman.</u>

MY PENIS
<u>CANNOT</u>
GET AROUSED
LOOKING
AT WOMAN'S BODY.

A vagina, a labia, a clitoris, doesn't move my Caucasian wiener.
It will stay 3-4 inches and not grow AN INCH if I look at one.
Even if I jerked off, I can't maintain an erection firm enough to finish.
That is literally IT.

MY DING-DONG
DOESNT GET LONG
FOR SOME WOMAN IN A THONG.

MY GOD.

So, barring all eternal death threats (which by the way are completely silly and ultimately meaningless)
I can't get a stiffy looking at pictures of tits and poontang.

Because I don't want to lick or flick down a clitoris... So I'm going to hell.

Your "god" hates me because I don't wanna stare at some big ole' JUGS
or finger doodle a woman's pleasure box.

WOW.

WOWWWWWWWWWWWWWW

You see how stupid that sounds.
It is really THAT SIMPLE, but you dumb dumbs have made it THAT DIFFICULT on other people.

But people have taken their own life and been killed because they wont put their hot dog inside of a moist whoo-hah.

It sounds funny, but it's something dead serious
and too many good people are now dead because of it.

IMAGINARY GODS
have killed OFF REAL PEOPLE.

For example, there was a group of kids that took their own life for being gay between
2011 - 2015 ish.
And for every month, another child who was gay, ended their life on earth.

Go google it. Im not doing the legwork for you.
You can read their lives or not. It doesnt matter at this stage.
Kids writing these suicide notes about how they were sorry people were ashamed of them
and hanging themselves or blowing their brains out with a gun they took.

FAGGOT COCKSUCKER QUEER
HOMOSEXUAL FREAK
GOING TO HELL
GOD HATES THEM
DOOMED!
!!!!!
(by the way, I don't take your try-hard words or YOU people seriously /// At
all)

Let's just take a quick look exactly what your anger causes and creates.

Brandon Elizares (June 2012) was found dead by his brother
after overdosing on pills from being bullied at school by his
peers for two years. Problems at school escalated when his peer group threatened to
burn and shoot him for
being gay. Before his death, he placed all of his awards and
trophies around his room and left a note that read "My name is
Brandon Joseph Elizares, and I couldn't make it. I love you guys

with all my heart." He was 16 years old. 💀

Jack Reese (April 2012), another victim of anti-gay bullying
from inside of his school, took his own life. His hobbies,
according to his obituary included: "He (Jack) was learning to
speak Japanese and loved anything to do with Japan. He was

also very good at drawing and photography." He was 17 years old. 💀

James Corey Jones (May 2012), a Minnesota Teen who jumped to his death after suffering from depression and constant taunts regarding his homosexuality and threats of people who had picked on him at school. His father, Jay Strader, said this about him: "He said all of his life people picked on him. He'd still try to keep his head up at school, but then he'd come home and be really sad about it. He just got really depressed about it because the other guys weren't

accepting him." He was also 17 years old. 💀

Eric James Borges (January 2012), an aspiring filmmaker from California, took his own life, after being a contributor to the Trevor Project, an organization which seeks to stop suicide among LGBT youth, he left a note that read " My pain is not caused because I am gay. My pain was caused by how I was

treated because I am gay." He was 19 years old. 💀

Kenneth James Weisuhn (April 2012) took his own life, after being the target of a hate group on Facebook surrounding his identity as a gay male. He was found dead by his family. He was

14 years old. 💀

Philip Parker, (January 2012), also fourteen, hung himself in his parents bathroom after reaching out to his mother saying "please help me" before taking his own life because of constant harassment for being homosexual in Tennessee. His death was followed by Jacob Rogers (December 2011), another Tennessee teen who had taken his life one month before Philip Parker. Jacob Rogers, 18, had dropped out of school, because "He started coming home his senior year saying 'I don't want to go back. Everyone is so mean. They call me a faggot, they call me gay, a queer." His friend had reported before he took his life. After both of these tragic deaths, the stunned community took up a pledge to start a state founded Equality project which quickly gained thousand of signatures in honor and memory of these two boys deaths. 💀💀

Asher Brown texas teen shot himself in the head with a 9 mm Beretta because of the constant bullying and teasing at his school. He was thirteen years old. Rafael Morales, taunted at his school for being openly gay, was found hanging over the side of a bridge. He was fourteen years old. Raymond Chase, culinary arts major; He was the fifth gay youth to commit suicide in a three week period in his area. He was nineteen years old. 💀💀💀

Justin Aaberg, a student of Anoka Highschool, hung himself out of shame for being gay. He was the third student of that district to take their life because of sexual identity. He was fifteen years old. Billy Lucas, an Indiana Teen was discovered dead in the family barn after hanging himself. It was reported by the media that he was bullied at school and called a "Fag," even though he had never officially come out to anyone. He was fifteen years old when he killed himself. Carlos Vigil, from New Mexico, before taking his own life, wrote on his twitter account "The kids in school are right, I am a loser, a freak and a fag and in no way is that acceptable for people to deal with. I'm sorry for not being a person that would make people proud." He was seventeen years old. Jamey Hubley, Seth Walsh, Josh Pacheco, Jadin Bell and Jamey

<u>Rodemeyer</u> were among others who also took their own lives that made global headlines. 💀💀💀💀💀💀💀💀

You religious people ACTUALLY speak of God?

I say, God Damnit how could you do this to a bunch of children?

Imaginary gods
kill REAL PEOPLE

I SAID WHAT I SAID

TYPE IN THEIR NAMES. THESE WERE REAL souls
This isn't some "Sob Story" with a fictitious number thrown in,
this is a real group of KIDS.

When your beliefs hurt others,
your beliefs need to be challenged
(and I'm sorry - someone has to say it - ultimately smacked)

Period.

We're not talking adults, we're talking young kids that hadn't even hit age 16. 12 year olds.

Awful. And Terrible.

BRUH, they couldn't get a boner for Bethany or Brenda,
and they socially ostracized to the point of DEATH
because of it.
………..

So think about this, Going back to the dissertation on human attraction, If I cant get
hard looking at a c*nt, or a twat, or whatever vulgar, crude, rude or SHOCKING
word you want to refer to those anatomical parts as,
How am I going to have sex with said orifice, if thats all I need to do for God to
"love" me and be acceptable.

HEY IDIOTS.
LIKE HELLO- --------

You cant fornicate someone with a soft cock.

HELLO.

U CANT DRILL A HOLE ---
WITH A LIMP PYTHON

You can sure as hell try but thats gonna be awkward and laughable.

You really think your deity cares whether I have a Va-china or a banana in my
mouth?
Thats like saying the President is worried whether I have decaf or regular coffee for
breakfast.

I think God and the president have bigger things to worry about
and SPEAKING of big THINGS
So if I lick balls *which I have* Im going to spend the rest of my eternity on fire.
THAT SOUNDS SO STUPID ====
YOU PEOPLE DONT HAVE TWO BRAIN CELLS TO RUB TOGETHER,
I SWEAR TO GOD,
YOUR GOD, AND EVERY GOD. THE GOD OF EGYPT, THE GOD OF ALLAH

Makes Angry Goat Noises

Even if I was sorry - which I'm not - got down on my knees, prayed and repented,
held the rosary, tightly, I still wouldn't be able to bed a woman.

There is no moment in time - that is remotely possible - where I'm NOT gay.

Even if I'm not having "gay sex" (By the way, it's just sex lmao)
Even if I'm not having gay sex.....I'm STILL GAY LOL.

AND Do you really think God wants a homosexual man or ANY MAN to subject
himself to that kind of embarrassment and shame?
Trying to put it inside a chick's mound but it wont get up. REALLY???

Imagine the gayest man you've ever met, like SUPER FLAMIN GAY, and then try
and imagine him going down on a female.
Yeah, it's not happening and WE BOTH know it.

You're dumb.
Like stupid dumb.
Not even funny dumb.
But more like you are a dumb-ass.

Me not getting hard for vagina, is seriously not a big deal at all, but its been turned
and made into the biggest HISTORICAL deal ever.

It has nothing to do with hating women - UM clearly not, since my own inner circle
has always been nothing but women. Feminine Energy has been whats been
AROUND me my wholllllllllllllllllllle Life.......... GO look at any photo of me and
it's ME surrounded by SIX GIRLS. RIP.
It has nothing to do with not having a strong male figure in my life - I grew up
around politically incorrect NRA, Rodeo loving classically masculine MEN
It has nothing to do with being abused, assaulted, ETC... Fill in the blank with

whatever crazy assertion,belief,idea thats been heard before.

The thing is, I can tell you exactly when I knew I was gay, before I understood what that meant in society.

When I was six, I saw the naked statue of David. In an Encyclopedia. (lol)
Before the days of Wikipedia.
And I couldn't stop looking at his hanging phallus AND his marbled Test-ickles
I was utterly captivated.
It was beautiful and whimsical and somehow powerful looking ALL at the same time.
Oh God, I was in LOVEEEEEEEEEE

I knew I liked that from THAT age.

flaps wrist into the air GAY

The carnal, sexualized light went off then.

I knew, in that deep, type of KNOWING.

THEN When I was eight, when the internet was just taking off, I searched for "Big Hairy Wiener." Those exact words.

Big.
Hairy.
Wiener.
I mean. LOL.
       ....MY DUDES I WAS ALWAYS GAY.

I seriously googled - Big Hairy Weiner.
LMAOOOOOOOOOOOOOOOOOOOOOO

What Im saying is - in the least arrogant way I can - everything ANYONE has ever said or thought around this issue has been wrong, in so many different kinds of ways.

I cant get a boner for a bitch. Why should I even feel sorry or hate myself for that?

Big deal.
Big whoop.
Oh my flipping GEE OH DEE (GOD)
WHO ACTUALLY cares?????
Get it through your SMALL brains.

Let's do this logically. Okay.

Seeing a dick makes my dick HARD, which would make my boyfriends dick HARD, because he likes dick too.

Its not that HARD 2 UNDERSTAND.

The quality of my life has been reduced,
and things have been made so incredibly HARD ON me
just because I get hard ons for a dude.

WHATTTTTTTTTTTTTTTTTTTTTTTTTTT

It really has nothing to do with ass, although thats where everyone gets hung up on, and I didnt need to make an ass of myself to explain all of this.

If you put a photo of a woman in front of me, better yet,
If an actual naked woman was standing before me - the most physically perfect and beautiful lady ever - great tits, round ass, aesthetically beautiful face and hair, never seen a double cheeseburger before, perfect figure, I STILL wouldnt be salivating and struggling to control myself like a straight man.

Nothing would be happening inside my head or inside my blood vessels of my other head.

Even if she touched me, I'm not getting hard.
Nothing is going to happppppen

Nothing.

There is no arousal looking at a woman, not because I think vagina is gross - I don't - it doesnt look like anything because there is NOTHING down there.

It just doesnt excite me ENOUGH to allow me to get an erection
SO get off my ass
with all your phony ideas about homosexuality and what it means.

When I look at a vagina, something is missing.
There's nothing there. ERROR ISSUE WITH GENITALIA!
It's two floral, skin flaps.
It's missing something important.

AND THAT SOMETHING IS A BIG DICK!

Thats it. Thats being gay.
In a nutshell.
Let people bust a nut.

GUYS have penises, and those penises have to become erect to have some enjoyment with them,
and then if they dont, you aint gettin nothin. (except a really awkward, never wanna talk about it again encounter, sorry I had too much wine and couldn't keep it up whiskey dick convo.)

Simple as that.

Were talking about DICK, but you dont have to be a dick to others because your book says so.

This book says be nice.

Oh and by the way, the long standing complaint that homosexuality at gay parades is too sexual... It has the word SEXUALITY in there.
Second of all, let people wear the unicorn boots and glittery boas all they want. Its one week of the year.
Stop raining on peoples parade.

Thank you.

Oh my god
Laughs

We just effortlessly bypassed over three thousand years of pain and ignorance.

You're welcome.
I really AM that talented.

We could have saved so much time,
and we could have saved SO MANY lives,
had that been said.

All that unthinkable SUFFERING because some man could ejaculate onto a clam plate.
Pathetic. Absurd. Insane.

BUT HOMOSEXUALITY ISNT NATURAL!!!!

MAN....It's <u>AS natural as waking up with morning wood poking out.</u>
MAN....It's <u>AS natural as getting an erection.</u>

(we get a THOUSAND of them everyday)
A !!!! THOUSAND!!! BONERS!!!

Listen. Even inSIDE my dreams, when I'm unconscious and not in control, drooling on a pillow with my mouth hanging open,
there has never once been a naked woman pop up and do something carnal. It's been sex with men all the way.
I'm not even conscious! My brain is, I'm passed the F out and still seeing COCK.
That's something far, far, FAR beyond the realm of daily human control.

There's never been some naked lady pop in on a stripper pole and go down on me as I made it rain in hundred dollar bill$$$$$

I would say being gay isn't natural, if I had some deep urges to bed a woman, but I've literally had naked guys walk around inside the shadow of my dreams.
THATS MY BRAIN CONTROLLING THE SCENE,
IM NOT EVEN IN CONTROL THEN.

NAKED MEN.
I've never even had a dirty thought for a woman.

NOT one.

You can threaten me with hell until you face turns every shade of the rainbow, quote every bible verse, speak in tongues,
but my dick still ain't moving an inch.

A SINGLE INCH.

And by the way - for the record - Sodom and Gomorrah was fake news.
That story is disgusting, imaginary, contradictory
and then the daughters end up BEDDING their own dad after getting him drunk on wine, after God kills Lot's wife and turns her into a pile of salt.

I'm not kidding. IF you said someone was turned into a pillar of SALT, you'd question TODAY if they needed to be placed inside a MENTAL ASYLUM.

This shit is STRAIGHT STUPID.

IM ARGUING.
WITH.
IDIOTS.

Just typing that out made me get a headache.

But they say were the gross ones.

Gross.

They EVEN said the world would end once gay marriage was legal.
HAS IT?
The absolute dramatics.

Remember when a legislator from my HOME state (Oklahomo)
said "Homosexuality is more dangerous to this nation than terrorist attacks. "

I CANT.

*REALLY? Jesus Bleepin****** Christ.*

Yes, two men holding hands is more dangerous than people flying planes into buildings and MURDERING THOUSANDS OF INNOCENTS???????????????????????????????????
You people are mentally helpless, so HELP me God.

erases the rest of the chalkboard
deep sighs

Oh well, now you know...

I dont want to hear anything else about it, ever again.

You read this and think.. Ok, I think I finally get it (homosexuality) now.

How people managed to psychologically and socially abuse their own children, making their offspring have deep seated issues FOR LIFE and tell them they were worthless and destined for hell, how parents and families looked down on their own biological creations and relatives, how people tortured each other into agonizing mental prisons -

That, I don't get.

"..., Well love the sinner, but hate the sin. "

NO. NO YOU DICKHEAD.
Let's STOP ALL THE HATE.
NO MORE HATE, GOD DAMNIT
IT'S NOT A SIN TO BE ALIVE!!!
PERIOD.
END OF STORY!

I would let you get away with saying Homosexuality is a SIN, if it wasn't NATURAL.
Murder, Rape, Lying, Hurting People - Those are all sins, no matter what definition of sin we want to use here; they include doing others wrong....

NOT being able to get a stiffy up in my pants for a lady ISN'T A SIN

That Lie,
That line ENDS HERE.

HOMOSEXUALITY ISNT A SIN,
HOMOSEXUALITY ISNT ANYTHING ELSE
BESIDES A NORMAL HUMAN (bitch, and animal)
STATE OF BEING,
NOT A STATE OF SPIRITUAL SUFFERING.

I sure have suffered enough on this earth though,
and I've certainly suffered too many fools.

--

Twirls hair

*So we've just taken immeasurable pain, suffering, tears, poisonous
contemptuous, anger of the last several thousand years and penultimately
solved the problem in less than 50 pages.*
Put it all into a cute, little pamphlet, for ya.
*Didnt need to attack anyone, didnt need to insult their gods or their sacred
beliefs, (not too much)*
didnt need to fight and argue.

*Sweet Mother Mary, I let everyone else make a total fool of themselves, fight
and argue.*
I may not be straight,
but now the record has been set straight.
Just put it on the table for all to see.
My work is done.
*Turns all the lights off, Leaves the classroom,
and quietly closes the heavy, old door behind me*

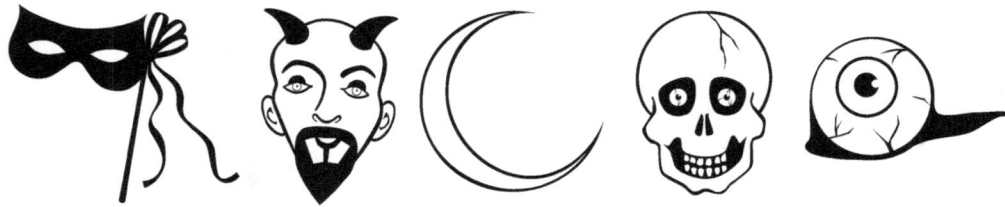

PART 2
ODDITY
THE EAGLE

I don't want a man inside me.
I don't enjoy anal sex.
I don't want a guy sticking his thing inside my ass.

NOW THAT'S A REAL SHOCKER

confused looks

"So wait, what do you do then??? I thought you were gay???"

IM AS GAY AS IT GETS, MARY
but I do not ENJOY backdoor entry.

I'm sorry, I hate it, I've tried to make myself enjoy it because it's what's
expected of ME, and being GAY,
but in no way do I like or want to engage in it.

Everytime, I've ever DONE it, I wanted to kill the guy.
Pure Murder.
He was having the time of his life, saying all sorts of dirty words,
and I was seriously thinking about snapping his neck.

Anal sex - isn't gross because of WHY people think it is, It's gross
because of HOW invasive it is.

I have space issues, and that is literally the most uncomfortable space
issue POSSIBLE.

I refuse, I flat out refuse.

I can't relax enough to enjoy it, even drunk, even on substances,
I still want the guy to GET OUT.

Listen, It's a strange thing indeed to be attracted to men
but to not want to be controlled by men.

Other gay men, have all these daddy fantasies and secretly love being
dominated and submissive,
but being controlled IS NOT my fantasy -
that is my NIGHTMARE.

Dip the rainbow flag in all black

I'm a completely different breed,
and I'm different when it comes to how I breed
and take a man's seed.
If that's too vulgar, at this point, after seeing everything else I've
written, I question if you know how to read.

I love guys, I love their body, I love their mind,

I go wild for masculine energy near me and ON me,
but I do not want MASCULINE energy shoved inside me.

I am a failure as a gay guy, because I'm so radically different
Lmao

I don't care how much I love Adam,
he is not sticking it up my exit door.

Okay, Okay so thats one big confession
Now I have another thats less sexual and more spiritual

You always hear the over-dramatic transexuals whining and crying
about how
"They were born in the wrong body" -- I'm a man stuck in a woman's
body, or I'm a woman stuck in a man's body… Whatever, Bob.

BOO Fricken HOO

I HATE BEING IN A HUMAN BODY, PERIOD.

Listen,
It wouldn't have mattered if I was born a man or a woman,
I'd Still BE TRAPPED inside some kind of flesh.

I do not enjoy being STUCK inside this skin and bone,
it doesn't matter either way if I have a penis or a Gash,
I have been annoyed to be stuck down here
SINCE I arrived. I sometimes hate being down HERE on earth.
Hate it. Would not recommend.
They had an entire war over skin coloring. AN ENTIRE WAR.
2 Stars on Yelp. PASS THIS PLANET UP.
GO SOMEWHERE ELSE. IT'S YUCKY.

I'm a raw spirit that should have never been put into flesh.

The body is a prison, bruh. Can I speak to a manager?

I live so far inside the mind,
I'm almost out of my body half the time,

points to the center of my skull

I'm inside HERE

I live inSIDE my head,
and not downstairs in my other head, like EVERY other guy.

GAY GUY OR STRAIGHT GUY,
it's all about whose gonna pleasure their mini me
Whose gonna rub it, whose gonna suck it

BO----RING.

Honestly, the truth is, I'm only here for a short while,
and I intend to use my time to create a better future
for those to come after me,
and then I'm getting the hell out of here.

Or Aliens, Abduct me.
Whichever happens first.
Death or Alien Abduction.

Part 1 - Scorpion, I went sexual
Part 2 - Eagle, I flew higher and went intellectual
Part 3 - Let's talk about God.

It's time to go up to heaven and meet the highest concept and idea of
them ALL.

It's time to burn through my star.

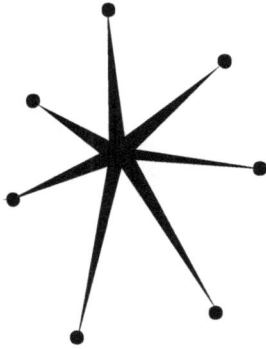

PART 3
PHOENIX

I love these people.
but I do NOT love their gods,
and their gods do not love me.

"You shall not lie with a male as with a woman; it is an abomination."

NEITHER THE HOMO-SEX-YOOALS WILL INHERIT THE
KINGDOM OF GOD NOR THE LIARS OR THE..."

I'm not even going to type out the rest, we've heard it ALL
before

Let me say it again:
I love these people.
but I do not love their gods,
and their gods do not love me.

Because I am very creative,
I believe in a creator

But not the God of Abraham, Jesus, Mohammed or the God of Moses.

Throws The Quaran, The Bible, and the Old Testament in the trash

(where they belong)
(sprinkles glitter on top and then sets it on fire)

It's not GOD I hate, it's their insane version that resembles more Angry
Middle Eastern Man than DIETY.

I knew I hated their God, when their God asked his first follower
to sacrifice his son. Yep, Nope. Can't stand that bullshit.

Disgusting.

When Abraham was told to take his child and kill him, to please God, I
deeply hated him.

Hate isn't strong enough of a word.

I found their Good God - to be the most evil thing ever come into existence.

Their God says we must FEAR HIM,
no bitch, you're gonna learn to FEAR ME.

The god of Abraham will harm no more innocent children after this.

It's true, I hated their God,
but I deeply resented/despised their devil, too.

I won't serve an evil man in the clouds,
anymore than I will be whipped around by some insane Red Devil
with pointy horns.

👹 ♱ ♱ ♱ BYE ♱ ♱ ♱ 👹

To HELL with them both. To hell with God and the Devil.

"If two men lie with one another, their blood shall be upon them."

No, the only blood I will have on my hands is those who oppose me
and wish me harm, in this life and in the next.

I will have their necks for trying to wish fire upon me.

If I'm really a flamer baby, don't you understand I'm immune to the
fire of hell.

Ah, Good Dad Jokes

When this life is finished, I don't want to go to heaven or hell.

Their Heaven SOUNDS like HELL to me.

Spending ETERNITY worshipping someone???
GOD NOOOO,
NOO PLEASE
I can barely get through two hours of church without wanting
to FLEE the premises

YUCK TIMES SIXTEEN
GROSS, DELETE

But then getting beaten and tortured by Lucifer doesn't sound too fun
either. Screw it.

Screw that, Screw Them,
And Screw Their Way of Thinking

*I find the biblical god to be a monster, I find Jesus to be insufferable and a
Drama Queen and his father, the equivalent of trying to deal with a terrorist.*

*"Whoever is captured will be thrust through; all who are caught will fall by
the sword. Their infants will be dashed to pieces before their eyes; their houses
will be looted and their wives violated." - Isaiah 13:16*

*"Happy is the one who seizes your infants and dashes them against the
rocks." Psalm 137:9*

*Yeah, I can quote a thousand other verses like this that make me wanna
chunk this book into the sea. Too much baby killing for me.*

Fucked up.
Anyway,
*Let's assume, shall we, that Everything the Bible has said is TRUE
and it IS the word of God, Gays will be lit into marshmallows, and God is
coming back to murder everyone who disagrees and save his chosen and
rapture them up.*

Lets assume, even though you know the saying about assuming.

coughs

GO back to genesis.
To the very, very, very, very start of all this stupid insanity.

Bible Pages Flip Backwards

THE ORIGIN STORY

Talking snakes, and Adam and Eve,
Forget Jesus, Forget Moses, Forget the Ten Commandments,
Forget a giant flood that never happened,
and let's just get back to basics.

A man and a woman, standing at a tree, masturbating, and K I SS ING

Even if Eve and Adam, had NOT eaten from that Tree
and EVE hadn't been BFFS with a talking Anaconda

Say they hadn't eaten from it, and Sin wouldn't have been put into motion…

Their children would have, and if not their children, their grand-children, or their great grand children.

God was waiting for humanity to screw up.
It was a setup, from the very get-go.

It was a scheme, the whole entire thing.

Had the two refused temptation, and gone on their merry way,
Their offspring would have given in. If not the first two, the next two,

or the two way down the line.

Some idiot was eventually going to screw up and eat an apple.

The cosmic drama of good and evil was rigged from Jump.

God isn't just evil on the grounds that he KNEW how events were going to play out, but introducing "sin" and letting kids die from cancer
and all matter of suffering because two idiots ate apples - is the highest, most unjustifiable crime ever.

I wont bow on my knees to your God or Devil,
because one is a dick, and the other is a straight UP asshole.

I will spit blood from cracked teeth at both of them,
if I'm ever in sight of either of those jerks.

God and the Devil both deserve to burn in hell for their actions.
Hell isn't strong enough.
They both deserve death

You see, I'm not rebellious to be edgy,
I'm rebelling because it's THE RIGHT thing to do

Im no atheist, but neither will I be counted as a believer.
I can't BELIEVE people would love something so messed up
But then, just look how MESSED up people are.

SHAKES MY HEAD

My soul isn't a pawn in the cosmic game for Yahweh or Lucifer.
I am not a bargaining chip between good and evil.

I will not bow to either. I will not give praise to either

I will not walk with the atheists, I will not sing with the Christians,
I will not draw pentagrams in a basement with sick satanists,
The cross, the muslim star, the Jewish whatever
ALL These symbols are so hateful and insane

I want out of this life, and then.

Truly then - will I be safe and free.

I want them all to know
Neither they,
Nor their Gods
can have my
SOUL.

If I don't want to be around them now,
why would I want to spend eternity with them?
Around them? Near them?

So where will I go? If the gates of heaven and hell are closed to me,
I suppose I'll enter Purgatory, and make it as my own.

A place for souls who were neither saints nor sinners,
I didn't ask to come down here,
but now that I'm here I'll make the best of the worst shit.

Up til the final moment, I've gotta be strong,
strong enough to defy them, strong enough to tell them "NO"
Strong enough to reject their ideas,
since they were weak minded (sick minded) enough to reject me.

The Individual must oppose the collective.
The outside man must pull off an inside job.

I was such a good kid,

but they treated me so bad.

I don't feel bad at all for balancing the scales.

Love a God that hates me? Worship... a "God" that hates me?
Believe in a book that ONLY LIES on me?

I. Don't. Fucki n. Think. So.

I wont respect beliefs that wont respect me,
I cant coexist with people that want me to be SET ON FIRE

I called part three
PHOENIX.

A PHOENIX, *because*

AN IMAGINARY CREATURE
<u>MUST KILL</u> AN IMAGINARY GOD

NOW - *BURN*.

ODDITYLER: Psychopath on a Warpath,
An ODD Boy, Getting rEVENge.

Curtain Drops

☮...when i die, bring fresh flowers up to my grave marker, so they all might truly say that I ROSE again

PART 3 IS THE PARTY
NOW SCREAM WITH ME

They lied their ass off about me,
Tonight get your ass in bed baby and lie with me
We'll only tell the truth,
(The naked truth)

Lets get into bed and have a conversation without any words (or
clothes on)

They called me awful names
Call me only by my name,
But I wont be anyones booty call
Pick up that phone
Tonight I dont want to be alone

But Dont ask, Dont Telephone

Every cell in my body wants you,

I'm giving your cell phone a ring-a-ling
Because tonight I've got an appointment
with yo ding-a-ling

HELLO! PICK UP! TELLING YOUR OWN KIDS YOU HATE THEM

BECAUSE THEY ARE GAY ISNT A GOOD IDEA
THIS IS YOUR WAKE UP CALL

I don't need to come out,
but I need you to come closer
Come on
Let's touch and get over our sexual hangups,
I survived them all,
Not another gay man that was hanging in a closet
Now get on top of me,
My well hung man.

I'm calling you for a night in
and I'm calling this world OUT
I serve levels of perfection,
they've never met someone who can so quickly talk about the power
of the erection
With some well placed puns,
Rub your pickle between my two buns.

Long gone are the days of the scholar,
Need a strong, WILD man to grab me by my collar

Since I can remember,
I've been PUSHING MYSELF
Need to find a man who will PULL ME CLOSE.

RING, RING
DO YOU HEAR THAT???
RING, RING!!!!
It's that nothing they ever said had a RING of truth to it,
For Fundamentalism,
There is fundamentally NO ROOM,
RING, RING
You may now kiss the groom,
Give me the Wedding RING
Baby, I do.

RING

in 2015, gay marriage was legalized, a major victory, but it's still a topical change. Tolerance isn't love. They may tolerate us, but they hardly love us, hardly want us.

And I hardly care what they want, believe or think.

You think, deep down, I'll ever truly forgive them for what they put me through? The ugliness? The whispers? The Yelling? The Attack on my very identity?
Not Hardly.

LOVE PECKED

PECKER
Gregory Peck's Pecker,
My sweet prince,
when doves cry,
Get me spread Eagle,
I'll give you a real Birds eye View

Saw pictures of her Ovaries,

but was furiously rubbing my rooster
to pictures of his big peacock, instead

Show me your little white lizard, Come on
Dont be a chicken, you should know by now
I don't date chicks
Sleeping Beauty, Finding Beauty in the Beast,
Spindles, lezzies and PRICKS

I used to be the ugly ducking
Then I became the Swan Prince
Lets talk the Birds and the bees
Let me see the phallus that sits between your knees
The male member that both ejaculates, hardens and pees

One flew over the cuckoos nest,
Ill rattle their cages, and ruffle some feathers
These rhymes will be one for the ages
Now I go with the sages,
As wise as an owl
Pissing people off,

is a real hoot.

You'll never see me looking at a woman's hooters,
or doing night-time transactions with her cooter

Jim Crow
Right Wing, Left Wing
Let's get political, Lame ducks
Let's get physical
Let's get Levitcal, you stupid fucks
ILL MAKE THEM EAT CROW
I'm one of the very best,
Don't ya know?

(With well placed words,
I can make them hysterical)

My words will all fly over their heads,
Gonna make this book FLY off the shelf

ERRORS, CLERICAL
The religious opinion of homosexuality
has always
been one for the birds.

PRACTICING MY HOMOSEXUALITY
I don't need to practice much,
I can just wing it.
Black Swan / Do me on the lawn
They'll never catch me,
Ill lead them on a wild goose chase.

Im about to cook their goose

You thought you could take me down,
You're a silly goose,
And I'm holding the noose.

I can't help that I love to CHOKE a man's chicken.
Now get away from me with all your awful bible verses,
YOU BIRD BRAINS

CAW CAW

Hah- Hah.

4th year RAVENKLAW

If you think Im done,
dont count your chickens before they hatch.
Don't care what you have to say, I ain't ever licking a snatch
THIS IS JUST THE FIRST BATCH.
Cooked this eggy up straight from scratch.

I'm watching you like a hawk right now.

I know what you think about me,
I know what you believe
because a little muslim birdy told me.

Jesus flipped over the tables in the temple,
I'll flip you off from the temple inside my head
Now I FLIP YOU THE BIRD.

Bird IS the word.
And the early bird really does get to suck on my worm.
I hope I make you people reading this cringe and SQUIRM.

I WANT your wood
I WANT your Pecker

If I fell asleep at work,
would that be considered my dream job?

If I sang in the shower,
would that be considered a soap Opera?

DANCE WITH ME, YOU STUPID MOTHERFUCKERS

CAW-CAW
CAW-CAW

(Hah-Hah, Hah-Hah)

Big Bird,
Big Dick,
Big Bank Account
Big House,
Big Life,
After I had to hear all their BIG FAT LIES

Christians wanna share the "Good News"
Well baby, I got some REAL bad news

I dont have to believe your lies,
NEWSFLASH
From saying any of this,
They looking shocked as hell
CAMERA FLASH

INTO THE LAKE OF FIRE,
Why WATER or dumb yourself down
When you could make a SPLASH

Their beliefs are trash
These born again babies
Have diaper rash
Promising me Hell
Lookin like a HeatRash
Writing this to earn some quick cash
Sounds like its gonna be another smash
I like Weenie and Not a Gash
Give em Whiplash
I'ma skip the Backlash
Bat my eyes,
lose an eyelash
Going head to head

In a cultural CLASH
Guys make me rock hard
Rockin out in these pages like Slash

Offensive AND bold
Im quite Brash.

Check yo self before yall believers wreck yoself
U're headin for a crash
Ive heard your ideas all before,
Not interested in your Old or New Testament Rehash
Burn it all down,
Leave em like Pompeii
Sitting in ASH
Wrote this in under 10 minutes,
Can do this in a flash
Thinking about what I should say next
While Stroking my Mustache.
Backspace, Enter, Period, Delete
Forward Slash

Gluteus Maximus

A senile senate
Homo Erectus,
Republicans in Rome,
Democrats in Damascus,
Bastards in Bethlehem
Masc for Masc
Sit on my spear, and suck it
I'll wrestle you to the floor
and show you my backdoor

Amphetamines in the Amphitheater
The Crowd goes Roar
The Angry Lion bares his teeth for more
Blasphemous UPROAR
Doth Quoth the Raven,
Forevermore.

As one door closes,
their mind closes another
CLOSE MINDED
WEARING NO CLOTHES
YOU THINK IM TALKING ABOUT MY BODY BUT
ILL SHOW YOU MIND.
I'll SHOW YOU A CREATURE
I'll SHOW YOU A LEGENDARY BEING

An eye for an eye,
He pulled out - of what is known as - the brown eye
and finished near my Blue Eye
It damn nearly gave me Pink eye,
I know you're rolling your eyes,
I know you're giving me the stink eye
I'll fight you, give you a black eye
(in the USA, might not be safe if you're a black guy)
IN AMERICA, OH SAY CAN YOU SEE
I've got all eyes on me
Men are my eye candy
You killed 2many of MY kind,
CANT YOU SEE??

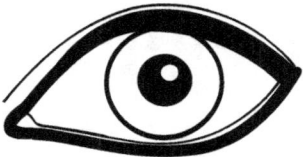

So I'll kill you with kindness
I'll show you how to TURN THE OTHER CHEEK
THE OTHER BUTT CHEEK
KISS MY ASS
BECAUSE THIS ONE IS AN EYE FOR EYE
I bet this strange book was a real eye opener

I've been watching you
with eyes in the back of my head
Talking about private things
In the public eye

TIRED OF ALL THE BULLSHIT
SO I HIT A PERFECT BULLSEYE
Im a bat out of hell,
But I can cuss someone out and not even bat an eye
Eye of the Hurrican,
Eye of the Tiger
Cat Eyes,
Now feast your eyes on my next move.
I can keep going
for as long as the eye can see.
Will I ever truly forgive them?
Eye really don't think so.

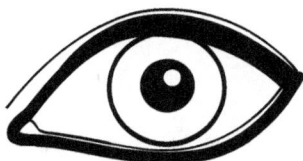

Private eye,
I've got my eyes on your privates
DICKTECTIVE,
Let's get to the bottom of this.

Let me inspect
what has now (obviously) become erect.

UNDER COVER LOVERS,
GET UNDER THESE COVERS
IVE GOT OVER THREE THOUSAND YEARS OF BULLSHIT TO FLY PAST
WEVE GOT A LOT OF GROUND TO COVER

IM TIRED OF THEM AND THEIR IDEAS
I would love some sleep,
JUST SHUTUP
AND LETS GET SOME SHUD-EYE

Wrote this in 2020,
to symbolize perfect vision,
but (on religious hatred) I don't think that we
will ever see

eye to eye.

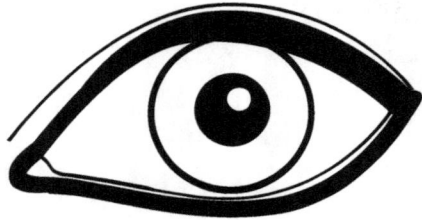

DEATH REBIRTH SEX AND SECRETS
WOMEN AND THEIR BEST FRIEND FAGS
RED FLAGS, RAINBOW FLAGS
AMERICAN FLAGS

The only document that shall control my fate,
as a citizen, OF THIS COUNTRY,
IS THE CONSTITUTION

NOT CHRISTIANITY,
NOT ISLAM,
NOT THE TWENTY COMMANDMENTS,
NOT THE 900 VIRGINS

THE
CONSTITUTION.

Wind on my face,
and all their bastard gods are dead,
No angels or demons to interfere
anymore with me being a human -
The way it should have always been

They thought I was gonna fly the freak flag,
but tonight,

I proudly fly the American Flag

Not all the colors, Not the rainbow,
Just three very specific colors,

RED WHITE AND BLUE

Without America,
I couldn't have done ANY of this
My freedom to speak against them
was CONTINGENT and hinged upon my citizenship here.

I would have been killed or tortured or jailed
anywhere else

LAND THAT I LOVE
WHERE I LIVED THROUGH SO MUCH HATE

They say Christ died for my "sins,"
but I don't give a single GOAT about him.

I only care about the soldier
who DIED for my FREEDOM.

Those souls who gifted me the ability to do and say ALL this.
The freedom that gifted me THIS VOICE.
Thank You, Eternally.

Christs blood did nothing,
The soldiers blood gave me the FREEDOM to do this:

AMERICA,
AMERICA,
THANK YOU

kisses the Winding Dirt Oklahoma Roads
Never knew I would have to fight against so many dirtbags
and douche-bags.

They thought they were gonna see the freak LGBT flag,
tonight I wave only the American Flag.
13 colonies, 12 disciples, 1 Country

Atheists, jews, muslims, Hindus and christians
all are gonna say I crossed the line,

Aiming at you with my magic crossbow
On these cultural crossroads
Caught up in the crossfire
Writing this took ten years,
My cross to bare
has been born.
Cross my heart,
and I Hope to live.
Dressed only In Crucifixes,
Tonight I'm going to cross-dress,
I've still got more words to give.

Born of a Mad Sagitarius
and Of an intense Scorpio
The Archer and the Stinger
Either way, you're gonna feel pain from me

So I take this Arrow
and Aim at the center,
Of all these issues,
I pray To a power higher than God,
and I release these sharp words
Along the arrow of time.

Through ALL of the Bullshit.
.
.
.

...

A Perfect Muthafuckin' Bullseye.

Line by Line,
Standing in the frontlines,
Writing this on a deadline,
Going as fast as I can before time makes my heart flatline,
Making my family mad,
OOPS! THERE GOES MY DOWRY FROM MY BLOODLINE
HERE COMES THE NEXT PUNCHLINE
Im trying my best,
THROW ME A LIFELINE
Did this in under 1 week,
Published on a timeline
My writing is top of the line,
I love naked men's ding dongs
and thats just the BOTTOM LINE

Leaving writing behind, for science
Social science for Pure sciences,
I'm already way on down the line
Will I have any more books coming down the pipeline?
Dont know,
but I'm almost there to the finish line
This isnt my line of work,
I dont like being in the line of fire,
much less their THREATS of a lake of fire

I've done a knockout job,
wrote it all hook line and sinker
Some of it was serious,
Some of it was funny,
So Whose line is it anyway?

Is he on drugs,
Is he snorting lines?
Between creative + crazy...
I know how to certainly blur the line.

Dont care about Democrats,
Dont care about Republicans,
Dont care about Independents,
WONT WALK ANY PARTY LINE
MY MESSAGE IS A REAL
POWERLINE

Wrote it all while Offline,
and Had it published, marketed and sold ONLINE

We're already coming to the end of the line
This was...

(...wait for it...)

The.
Storyline.

EVEN THOUGH I AM GAY
I MOVE ONLY IN STRAIGHT LINES

This reality is a MADHOUSE
So much pent up anger
residing in the penthouses
Is there a disturbance in your residence?
Write it
with the cadence
of dissidence
Distract them, while I clean up all the semen strains evidence
With one of his nuts in my mouth,
I'm a nutcase living in a
NUTHOUSE
Finally could get married,
Take me down to the courthouse,
They were all SO full of shit,
In and out
of the Outhouse
Catty words,
I've got them all in the doghouse

Not another gay man,
You won't catch me in any shady, seedy bathhouse
Without a publisher
I don't need to sign with any publishing-house
and that includes randomhouse and penguinhouse

Working in a little restaurant
In the front of house,
Trying to save up enough
to finally leave the minimum-wage poorhouse
Made this meal, Homemade,
After this book,
Baby, I got it made.
Sign the tax documents + Make me your spouse
They all ingloriously lied,
Now let's get gloriously laid.
LAY THE PIPE DOWN ON ME, BABY
Check my plumbing,

Oh God,
I think I'm comi---

Changing their tune,
I'll have them all absolutely humming.
Once lived like I was slumming, Dirt Poor
These words are filthy,
But someday I'll be filthy rich
Rich enough to own a boathouse,
I'll be what's known AS the man of THE house
And that's the way the cookie crumbles
LOL, Bitch It's Toll House
I'm an angel from hell,
Burning down this MOTHAF***CKIN house

living room, attic, basement, bathroom, bedroom,
laundry room, dining room,
MASTURBATION UP IN THE MASTER-BEDROOM
A place to fornicate for two aroused Grooms
Tv Room, Staircase, Study
motions finger
Come a little closer, buddy

That's enough out of you, Buddy
NOW GET THE HELL OUT OF MY HOUSE
DONT EVER TRY AND COME THROUGH MY BACKDOOR

Through all of that heavy darkness,
I had the strength, the willpower to be a lighthouse.
I WILL FOREVER BE REMEMBERED AS A POWERHOUSE

THROUGH ALL THAT DARKNESS, I WAS A LIGHTHOUSE
THROUGH ALL THAT DARKNESS, I HAD THE STRENGTH
TO BE A P O W E R H O U S E

PHALLUS IN WONDERLAND

No job,
but she still gave him a hand :)
He poured the offerings of his phallus
into her triangular chalice
She was the new Aynn Rand
Writ Against the backdrop
of Biblical Malice
There we two Rabbits, in total
On Hugh Hefner's PlayBoy Bunny Palace,
A Black Rabbit
And the Story of the Anxious, Running White Rabbit
In the Fantastical Story of Alice
For them both, a jack rabbit toy
Ive said somethings bad,
Dang Nab bit
Writing controversial things
to offend the nuns of this world,
I have a bad habit
They all lie, religiously
and cant get their stories straight
Habitually,
Socially Things will completely change,
Eventually.

Watch out!
That COCKSUCKER is a bloodsucker
He wants to suck on your ------------ blood, bud

He's a tramp, He's a vamp
This is the time stamp,
With the bookmark of the beast.
I give you something to feast

Dracula with a wig becomes Count Drag-ula
Crazy like Caligula
Cookin Trouble up in the kitchen
Get the Spatulas

Now get the estrogen eggs,
And open up your legs.

BITE ME

Their words about gays really bug me,
Turn on the windshield wiper
Abrahamic, Middle Eastern Viper
American Sniper,
Dressed Sharp, you'll be the sharpshooter
You might not be all that straight, but you're a real straight-
shooter
Right to bare arms... now let me bare my legs and my BODY!
Come in guns a blazin, triggering them, talking about reproductive

things with the sexxx pistols

Bop it, Twist it, Pull it!
Yin-Yang, Let me show you how to keep grip on a dude's Hairy Wang.

They say you bite the pillow,
but tonight they'll all be biting the bullet.

Smoked 2 much pot and lost the plot
And When I lost my mind,
I was the gay male
they tried to keep restrained in a straight jacket
I escaped, Insane, and In Pain
I won my victory
after they talked ALL that smack, lettuce get in the sack,
and I'll play with your sac, toss my salad from the back.
I'm a total wisecrack,
never been one to hold back
Obsessed with the future,
I don't look spend my time looking back.
Can handle them,
don't worry about the push back
I'll flash them
while I have these psychological flashbacks
Get the KODAK
Wrote this in a paperback.
Like music to my hears,
My first book was titled "A sodomite's soundtrack." (ASS)

But I changed it to the Direction of your Erection,
Because I liked the playback.
Im an artist, drawing it out now,
but this one has no drawbacks.
I can safely say I kicked their asses,
and can now enjoy a nice little financial kickback.
Years ago, I killed the blonde,
and since I was about 15 - my hair has been kept a dark, jet black.
Never been afraid to speak up and stand up,
You might wanna standback,
I've done something I can't take back,
And I know there is no going back.

No matter what happens, going forward,
from every edge of defeat
I've got the resources and the resilience
to bounce back.

Won't let anyone ride my coatails,
you won't be getting an intellectual piggyback
I've been coached how to conduct myself,
you bitches can all give me five and do a jumpingjack
Like a butterfly, like a bee
YellowJack

Dont worry about their negativity,
I've already gotten enough positive feedback
Truth is, I'm talking about sex
but I ain't no nymphomaniac
This was just my first angle of attack.
Aquarius, Water carrier
11th sign of the zodiac.
Often thought as a megalomanic.
But Always a brainiac.
Pick up an almanac
I can go my own way,
off the beaten track

You've been beaten, NOW BEAT IT
I'm leaving English literature
to work behing the scenes in science,
there is my biofeedback

Gotta get this message filtered into the public water supply,
somehow, without watering myself down,
might use colorful words
and paint a picture with some watercolors
But it's easy for me,
since I am Aquarius,
The Water Carrier.

A COLORFUL MAN WITH COLORFUL WORDS
CALL ME THE NEW LANGSTON
HUES

They say I'll be lit ablaze
down in the lake
of fire
Strong words for me,
I had to fight back
when the situation of my existence became dire.

Yes I know what they think about me
and
I don't care.
I only want to become a millionaire.
and see my face in the pages of Vanity fair.
I'm a social climber,
and this is just the first step up of that infamous stair.

Put your hardware inside my software - dirty cumputer
I BOLDLY questioned their ideas
With this brief questionnaire
They were all full of hot air,
but I was capable of walking on sunshine, and walking on air.
They showed me hate,
but writing was always my first love affair
I want everyone to hear this,
From Denmark to Delaware
and even farther,
Elsewhere.
America has a lot of problems right now,
from tolerance, Democrats and Republicans Hating Each other,
to healthcare
everyone acts like a belligerent child,
They need to go to daycare, but nobody can afford childcare
The American Dream
is sometimes a Nationalistic Nightmare
Here we are, Somewhere
Where are we going, Nowhere
Where is Everyone at, Everywhere
Their, They're and There
It'll all be okay... There, there, there
This was fun,
Until next time,
Take care.

Did you see what I did there? X-RAY
This 1 was X-Rated
I'm not an X-man,
just a gay man,
Gambit was always my favorite man,
and this was my actual gamble.
I loved the x-men
but never found myself attracted to any gay men,
just straight men.
Men have always been my Achilles (high) Heel

On, shall I ramble.
Leave their ideas in a real shamble,
to work against me,
they'll have to be quicker than me and scramble,
Now scram,
This is just the preamble.

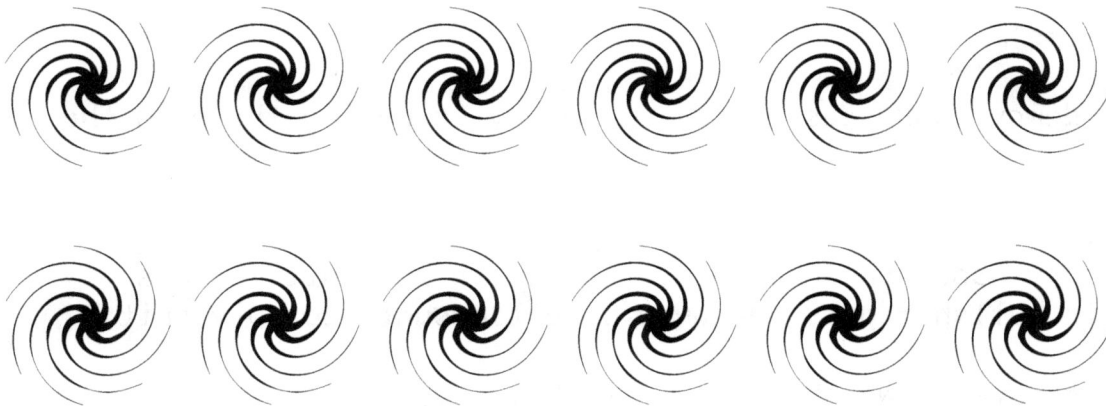

I've taken a difficult subject that people couldn't explain in
thousands and thousands of books.
I did this - effortlessly - in less than 100 pages.
The beekeepers and gatekeepers of the literary world can suck a
fat one.
A chode, a load...
Lastly, King Solomon - dude from the bible - had 700 wives and
THREE HUNDRED concubines (pretty semen vessels and you know it)
and you jerkoffs… you jerkoffs actually tried to stop me from
having ONE husband.
ONE HUSBAND, BUT HE (that crowned dickhead) CAN HAVE 1,000 WIVES.
BITCH…

Rips hair out
I'm going to La-la-La-Lose it!

I really hate you all. What IN the hell. LOL.
Of the same sex,
but this is NOT the same old STORY

# of Adam and Steve,

Could have saved this world all the time and trouble,

by saying my willy just won't **GET BIG** for Eve.

pause the present moment

Stops time

Turns sideways and sees a kid, whose gay, standing there in the future

Hey kid,
Don't worry about these people, with their bullshit beliefs
and their bullshit gods, because it all amounts to holy shit.

You don't have to worship the shit they say,
You don't have to do any of the things they say,
You don't have to live the way they shout and scream
and when they're not screaming, they hit you with constant silent disproval.

You're not going to hell.

Go live your life,

go be **happy**,

go and be <u>**gay**</u>.

Being gay USED to mean to be happy. SO GO BE GAY.

I'll handle them + their gods.

    I'll use my life to improve the future quality of yours.

Returns back to the present moment

Breathes in, deeply
Stares straight ahead at the keyboard

While The religious people wait for the world to end,

We're gonna make this world a better place.

There is a world of difference between me and them.

THEY PROMISED ME FIRE
ITS TIME TO OPEN FIRE
ITS TIME TO RETURN FIRE

BURN THEM, PHOENIX OF MY HEART

The. Fucking. End.

- Ending, Hidden Scene

Come with me, naked male lover
into Purgatory

It is a dark desert here,
empty of Gods and Devils
No flames, No bright lights
No white mansions of God,
No red Fires of The Devil
No angels, no demons,
no other loudmouth people for miles.

It's peaceful; it is quiet.
and we can be forever away from ALL of THAT.

Listen,
I tried so extremely hard, I gave it everything I ever had
..but
If I still failed in the task of destroying their Gods,
If I didn't have the strength to destroy
heaven and hell, if the gates of eternity still stand
If the creator and his most prized, fallen angel
still are at war for the soul of humanity,
Hold me,
and Make love to me on these dark sands.

Love me until time loses all meaning, love me forever
and the scars they left on me,
heal.

All I ever wanted was
 love. (and a lot of money depo$ited into checking)

*GOAT mask falls to the floor,
as I carnally rip off his belt and fling it to the side*

I'm tired of being a human being,
I'm tired of trying to impress these people that mean nothing
remind me with your hands
what it's like to be an animal
You are hard,
and my body is soft
and I love you.

I just wanted to be a lover,
and God made me a fucking fighter

I've let them see glimpses into my mind,
I've let them see my thoughts,
Take me to a place where no eyes can follow us,
where no eyes can judge us,
no eyes can plan to attack us,

eyes turn completely black

MAKE LOVE TO ME,
I HATE THAT THEY TOOK THE QUALITY OF LIFE AWAY FROM ME
I HATE THE FACT THAT THEY COULDN'T SEE I WAS A GOOD PERSON
AND THEY KEPT SAYING ALL THESE BAD THINGS
AND BAD BIBLE VERSES
AND THESE BAD PEOPLE WORSHIPPED BAD GODS

It's a good thing I was built tough.

There were no dances, no dinners,
JUST SHAME, HATE AND DISAPPROVAL
I HATE THAT IVE BEEN FIGHTING FOR SO LONG,

Born with the birth chord wrapped around my neck.

I HAVE been fighting - JUST TO LIVE - ever since.

- Tyler Lazarus Stump,
Written in the year Two Thousand & Twenty

OH!
Wait A Minute!!!!!
There actually IS one more crucial piece of data to be added into the log.
Something maybe even more important. How did I almost forget?

Because I'm not taking off my pants and showing you my wiener,
since A. How Awkward, my God and B. I'm not a porn star and THAT'S not my
vocation/occupation, but there is one actual thing that will convince you. At least
it should beyond a shadow of a doubt. Something less carnal and way easier to
speak of.

(The fact that I had to dedicate the very start of my writing career
to talking about Hard Penis and Wet Vagina actually deeply upsets me... RIP)

But It's the speaking voice. GAY VOICE. It's very real.

You know EXACTLY what I'm talking about.

Almost every homosexual has it, some to greater and lesser degrees.

We're NOT choosing to sound LIKE THAT.

UM ---- DEFINITELY. NOT.

WHO WANTS TO SOUND LIKE THAT????

I've wanted to rip my voice box out since I heard the horrid thing, but I'm stuck with it for life.

Sweet Baby Jesus, Gay voice is real and IT IS ATROCIOUS.
#TERRIBLE

Unless vocal modification becomes something real in the future (PLEASE)

Anyway, so you don't need to see my junk, or my ballsack, just listen to a gay man TALK. There is something there WAITING to be unlocked by scientists, I just know it.

YOU CAN LITERALLY HEAR THE GHEY, WHEN A GAY GUY SPEAKS. LITERALLY.

It's a final, definitive, incontrovertible proof that homosexuality is natural.
On a psychological, Sociological, and Biological level.
On a vocal level.
Every primal level that makes a person, a person.

That voice usually comes WITH the gay guy. Poor #tingz.
Me included.

I may not like my speaking voice, but the voice you're hearing inside here is 100% pure. I can change the world with it.

AND While I may be gay, I've finally set the record straight.

The Real, Final End

I want Christians, Nonsensical Jewish Law and fiery Muslims to know - I want them all to realize - to fully understand on every level of linguistic comprehension: to finally accept the fact that:

My LIGHT was stronger than their holy words, stronger than their mortal gods born from the Middle East and when the bell of death tolls out for me,

I will walk into the light,
To be reunited again with the very source of all things, to return to a power even higher than their almighty
Triumphant, knowing I challenged, head on,
A great spiritual darkness.

A monster of monotheism
A dragon of dogma
A mad bull of bullshit
Slayed + Staked with the sword of my spirit
On the journey of life

Evil PLAINLY masquerading as good.
Confusion calling itself clarity.
Mental illness calling itself by sanity
Hypocrisy deeming itself the holy
Of Holies.

When I stand before the god of all things, stripped of everything except the energy of my rebellious soul. it won't be Jesus in sandals and a cheap robe, or Mohammed bowing on a frayed rug in the desert but a force far beyond anything that has ever been conceived by any human mind.

That is the true god. Incomprehensible in scope

That is the hidden power I serve. Divine in radiance Beyond description, language shatters before it, both atheists and Christians will bow, but my knee will not bow to their false god in this life or the next. I will not serve the cross, I will not serve the muslim star and crescent. I can't bow down to evilness, I'm sorry. I won't.

I will not glorify human lies.

Anything else is fraudulence and ego run rampant
My light wasn't just stronger,
But that I was far stronger.
Stronger than everything they ever said and believed.

The abrahamic gods don't do GOD justice, and in the abrahamic gods name there has been too much injustice. Too much cruelty. Too much hate labeled as "love."

I cast a prophecy further than my life will be,
That the old will fall and the new shall rise
And rise up.

That there is a power even higher than God.
Until the final moment, I will defy them all, Jesus and the devil, symbols both angelic and demonic, men and women, gays and straights. I will defy all people and all gods. The world is not my final destination, I'm only a traveler.

This is not my home.
I'm running through the corridors of time
Towards the fields of eternity

And freedom

Of the reactivity and looming stinger of the scorpion,
Of the calculated eye, wing and claw of the eagle,
of the piercing scream, shriek and inferno of the Phoenix

OF PAIN,
POWER

AND GLORY

The Phoenix
An imaginary creature
Must challenge an imaginary god

They wanna have six marriages and five abortions
but yet STILL CALL ME THE SINNER?

You all can Go to hell.
It's like all these people that talk about God,
That need God,
are the most Ungodly people I've ever met in my life.

Those ugly ass bible verses and hateful words
aren't gonna crush my spirit,
it's all just words,
and I've got some words of my own.

ODDITY/LER

Out of the ruins of Sodom and Gomorrah,
A hope appears
from under all of the rubble
In the form of a boy.

Winks at the audience

www.ingramcontent.com/pod-product-compliance
Lightning Source LLC
Chambersburg PA
CBHW082012290326

41934CB00014BA/3318